100

QUESTIONS AND ANSWERS

ENERGIZE

YOUR FAITH

AND REIGN

ANDREW E. IGENE

authorHOUSE®

AuthorHouse™ LLC
1663 Liberty Drive
Bloomington, IN 47403
www.authorhouse.com
Phone: 1-800-839-8640

Unless otherwise indicated, Bible quotations are taken from the Authorized
of King James Version Text. Copyright 1963, 1965, 1968, 1970, 1971, 1973
by Finis Jennings Dake, Dake Bible Sales, Inc; Lawrencewille, Georgia.

Published by AuthorHouse 01/24/2014

ISBN: 978-1-4918-2654-6 (sc)
ISBN: 978-1-4918-2653-9 (e)

Library of Congress Control Number: 2013918220

Any people depicted in stock imagery provided by Thinkstock are models,
and such images are being used for illustrative purposes only.
Certain stock imagery © Thinkstock.

This book is printed on acid-free paper.

Because of the dynamic nature of the Internet, any web
addresses or links contained in this book may have changed
since publication and may no longer be valid.

The views expressed in this work are solely those of the author
and do not necessarily reflect the views of the publisher, and the
publisher hereby disclaims any responsibility for them.

DEDICATION

To my wonderful Lord and Savior Jesus Christ
Who has blessed and strengthened me
To shoot at my goal
Anywhere
From pole to pole.

INTRODUCTION

This is a rallying cry to the Church to return to the basics, to the very foundation of our most holy faith.

Why? Because the spiritual structure of the House is crumbling in several places, due to gradual erosion of foundational truths.

When the Lord spoke to me, a few years back, to . . . "Go" . . . . and get His people back to the "foundation," it really struck me as a challenge. I had observed the denigration of the foundations of our faith for years. And now, I received the mandate to do something about it.

But I had no idea how challenging it would be, until I started traveling to the nations on the mission field (as He had commissioned me)!

Truly, many church leaders have since abandoned the simplicity of the gospel and gone after "politically correct," populist fables on such basic truths as Salvation, the Blood of Jesus, Deliverance, the Prophetic Ministry etc.

As I travel and minister in churches, crusades, conventions and youth rallies, my heart is burdened because I see that many, many people are hungry and thirsty for the real, undiluted gospel.

I thank God for many pastors and other ministers in many places, too, who have not swallowed Satan's bait . . . who have not bowed their knees to Baal.

They are, indeed, co-laborers, inspiring the troop (so to speak), without compromise, Praise the Lord!

This book is a timely compilation of the most forthcoming questions and answers, starting with

—"What must I do to be saved?"

It is my earnest prayer that the wide-ranging topics covered here, will clear away the cobwebs of religious confusion in many hearts.

This is not a denominational message, it is Christ-centered, to the Body of Christ everywhere, to every nation!

Take some time, read and study through and you will be blessed. You will be inspired and edified.

This book will also bring deliverance to the lukewarm and unsaved.

I recommend it as an effective evangelistic tool, to reach out to those who are in the "highways" and "byways" of life, traveling different religious directions, seeking truth, without Christ.

Pastors, ministers, Bible School students and church workers will find it, useful and appropriate for these times.

There is revelation knowledge in the following pages, sent to bless you beyond your present testimony and make you more productive in the Lord's service.

O yes, it's time to energize your faith and reign in Christ!

CONTENTS

CHAPTER 1

CHAPTER 2

CHAPTER 3

CHAPTER 4

CHAPTER 5

CHAPTER 6

CHAPTER 7

CHAPTER 8

CHAPTER 9

CHAPTER 10

CHAPTER 1
Salvation

1.   What must I do to be saved?

Mk 1:15 . . . "*Repent and believe the gospel.*"

Mk. 6:12—"*And they went out and preached that men should repent.*"

Acts. 2:38—"*Then Peter said unto them, Repent, and be baptized every one of you in the name of Jesus Christ for the remission of sins, and ye shall receive the gift of the Holy Ghost.*"

Repentance, therefore, is the first step towards God.

Come to God and be sorry for your sins.

Take the blame for your life as a sinner.

Then, seek forgiveness. Jesus died on the cross; shed His blood to set us free from sin. Receive the good news, believe and thou shall be saved.

Mk. 16:15-16. "*And he said unto them, Go ye into all the world, and preach the gospel to every creature.*

"*He that believeth and is baptized shall be saved; but he that believeth not, shall be damned.*"

Receive the Lord Jesus into your heart and live by faith and praise Him for His mercies. Ask Him to come into your life . . . be your Lord and Savior.

This gospel is the "power of God unto salvation to everyone that believeth" (Rom. 1:16)! Believing the good news is the power to transform you from darkness, sin and shame to light, hope and newness of life in Christ.

To "repent" means "to feel regret or contrition . . ." or self-reproach for what one has done (sin) . . ." and then "turn from sin and dedicate oneself to walk the new life in Christ Jesus."

So you see, it is not enough to repeat the "sinner's prayer," you must pray candidly from your heart to the Lord. Tell him you are sorry for your sins. Thank Him for His Blood, shed at Calvary to save you from sin.

Ask Him to wash away your sins and iniquities, as He promised.

Ask Him to give you a new heart desirous to serve Him. Tell Him you want to be His child for the rest of you days.

Then, thank Him for His grace because you don't deserve it by your "works" or "good deeds," but by His grace! For it is the gift of God!

Receive Him into your heart, because He has answered your prayers (according to His word). He will not cast you out when you come to Him.

Rejoice for His salvation, the new birth and sins forgiven!

Get a good Bible-believing, Holy Ghost (holiness) church.

The Holy Spirit will order your steps, and you will grow in the Lord! (Amen)!

2 Cor. 5:17—*"Therefore if any man be in Christ, he is a new creature; old things are passed away; behold, all things are become new.*

The Spirit of God will enable you change your old habits; and create a hunger in your spirit for the Word of God, the deep things of God, as you "hunger and thirst" after Christ.

2. How can I know that I'm born again?

You have the assurance in your spirit that you are a child of God. It's called the peace of God "which passseth all understanding." **(Phil. 4:7)**

New life in Christ will be your testimony; loving the Lord and wanting to do His will in your life, will be your ultimate desire.

Moreover, the former passions of the world and its lusts will no longer be your past time.

The places you used to go will attract you no more; as you turn your life over to Jesus, the Messiah.

Old friends and the "former hang-outs" will fade off, as you discover more grace and love in Christ.

The Holy Spirit bears witness with your spirit that you are (now) a child of God.

Jn. 1:12—"*As many as received Him (Christ), to them gave He power to become the sons of God, even to them that believe on His Name.*" That includes you!

3. My church teaches that keeping the 10 commandments will save you at the last day. Is it correct?

No!

Your church is wrong in teaching that salvation comes through the keeping of the commandments. By our own strength and efforts, we cannot keep the commandments. That's the reason Christ died on the Cross and set us free from the curse of the law. Jesus now makes it possible.

By believing (and accepting) His finished work at the Cross, the Spirit comes into our lives and enables us to live a holy life acceptable unto Him. It is the Blood of Jesus that makes this possible, not our "sincere" religious rituals. Not our feeble efforts to keep the commandments without Christ.

Is. 64:6-"But we are all as unclean thing, and all our righteousnesses are as filthy rags . . ."! In our natural state (without Christ) all our "righteousnesses" (note the plural) are as filthy rags before the Lord.

Is 53:6—"All we like sheep have gone astray; we have turned everyone to his own way, and the Lord hath laid on him (Christ) the iniquity of us all" (Amen)!

Rom. 6:23—"For the wages of sin is death; but the gift of God is eternal life through Jesus Christ our Lord."

Rom. 4:6-7,—"Even as David also describeth the blessedness of the man, unto whom God imputeth righteousness without works,

"Saying, Blessed are they whose iniquities are forgiven, and whose sins are covered.

Verse 8—"Blessed is the man to whom the Lord will not impute sin."

Rom. 10:9—". . . If thou shalt confess with thy mouth the Lord Jesus, and shalt believe in thine heart that God hath raised him from the dead, thou shalt be saved."

Verse 10—"for with the heart man believeth unto righteousness; and with the mouth confession is made unto salvation."

Verse 13 . . . . "For whosoever shall call upon the name of the Lord shall be saved."

Do you see that? "Whosoever"!

That includes you, right now! The day of salvation is now.

4. What about other religions? Will they be saved?

Jn. 14:6—"Jesus saith unto him, I am the way, the truth, and the life: no man cometh unto the Father, but by me."

Acts 4:12—"Neither is there salvation in any other; for there is none other name under heaven given among men whereby we must be saved."

5. Will paying tithes and offerings qualify me for salvation?

While paying tithes and other financial contributions are to be encouraged in the church, such actions do not, by themselves, guarantee salvation.

Our works do not grant us salvation.

But after we are saved, our tithes, offerings and other acts of service and love become meaningful to the Lord.

Cornelius was "a devout man" .... he "feared God with all his house . . ." gave "much alms to the people" .... And "prayed to God always."

His religious commitment, morality, humanitarian credentials were very impressive by any standard.

Yet, salvation did not come to him by his works. He was directed by the angel to send for Peter (who came) and preached the gospel to him (to be saved) and receive the Holy Ghost (Acts 10:1-48)!

Titus 2:11—*"For the grace of God that bringeth salvation, hath appeared to all men. {But you must step forward, accept, and receive this salvation}!*

Verse 12—*". . . Teaching us that, denying "ungodliness" and "worldly lusts," we should live soberly, righteously, and godly in this present world; [we must deny ungodliness in real practical terms.]*

Verse 13—*"Looking for that blessed hope, and the glorious appearing of the great God and our Savior Jesus Christ; who gave Himself for us, that He might redeem us from all iniquity, and purify unto Himself, a peculiar people, zealous of good works."*

You cannot "buy" salvation with "tithes" and "offerings."

Be saved, then your tithes and offerings will have eternal significance.

6. Will shaking the preacher's hand save me?

No! Shaking the preacher's hand will not save you.

Only faith in the finished work of Christ at the Cross will guarantee salvation.

The precious Blood of Jesus still avails, not the preacher's hand-shake.

7. I am a faithful member of my church, blessed in material things. Isn't that proof that I'm saved?

No! Being blessed "materially" is no proof of salvation. There are many in the world who neither know our Lord Jesus, nor acknowledge Him. Yet they are rich in "material things."

Wealth in itself is no confirmation of an individual's spiritual condition.

Lk. 12:15—". . . . *For a man's life consisteth not in the abundance of the things which he possesseth.*"

To be saved, you must be "born again" **(Jn. 3:1-12)**!

Are you saved?

Are you born again?

Are your sins washed away by His Blood?

8. Elder, Deacon, Choir, Youth ministry, Women's Ministry etc . . . Are these not evidence of salvation?

Serving in these capacities do not necessarily mean that those involved are saved (born-again)! Yes, there are many people who are saved and serving in various levels in the church.

Being active in church programs, while commendable, do not equate to salvation. The question remains-

- Are you saved?
- Are you washed in the Blood of the Lamb?
- Are you sure you are His child?
- Do you have a personal relationship with our Lord Jesus?
- Can you truly say—"I am His and He is mine"?

9. I am saved. But my church doesn't teach "born-again." Do I continue to attend the church?

You need to grow in the Lord. Your church will not provide the necessary foundation for your spiritual growth.

Therefore, get a Bible-believing church (or fellowship) where you will meet other believers, for Bible Study, prayer meetings etc . . .

The Lord might still want you in your church, to lead others to Christ. But get somewhere else for real bible study & grow in spirit and truth.

He will lead you.

Be a witness for Him.

10. I'm a faithful member of my church, but I also go to "nightclubs" and have fun with my girlfriends. Why will my church loyalty not save me?

Church loyalty, per se, will not save you because salvation is not based on your works. Your acceptance and faith in the finished work of Christ at the Cross is the basis of salvation. When Christ lives in you, He will give you power (enablement) to live the "new life". The old life of "nightclubs" and "fun" with "girlfriends" will fade as the Lord becomes your Lord and Savior.

While church membership is fine, that alone, will not guarantee salvation.

11. Isn't God's grace sufficient even if I secretly retain some of my old lifestyle?

Rom. 6:1-2—*"What shall we say then? Shall we continue in sin, that grace may abound? "God forbid. How shall we, that are dead to sin, live any longer therein?*

12. How do I practically experience this newness of life in Christ?

Not by your strength but by the grace of God (available to whosoever believes).

Rom. 6:11—*"Likewise reckon ye also yourself to be dead indeed unto sin, but alive unto God through Jesus Christ our Lord.*

Verse 12—*"Let not sin therefore reign (dominate, rule) in your mortal body, that ye should obey it in the lusts thereof.*

Verse 13—*"Neither yield (surrender) ye your members as instruments of unrighteousness unto sin; but yield (surrender) yourselves unto God, as those that are alive from the dead and your members; as instruments of righteousness unto God.*

Verse 14—*"For sin shall not have dominion (rule, reign) over you: for ye are not under the law, but under grace.*

Verse 15—*"What then? Shall we sin, because we are not under the law, but under grace? God forbid.*

13. If I sin and repent, will God forgive me?

Yes. True repentance will bring forgiveness from the Lord. **Ps. 103:3**—"Who forgiveth all thine iniquities . . ."!

14. How can I be sure?

Because the Word of God says so.
God is truth and He cannot lie.

CHAPTER 2
The Blood of Jesus

15. Blood of Jesus as atonement?

Lev. 17:11—"*For the life of the flesh is in the blood . . . . for it is the blood that maketh an atonement for the soul*".

Mt. 26:28—"*For this is my blood of the new testament, which is shed for many for the remission of sins.*"

Eph. 1:7—"*In whom we have redemption through his blood, the forgiveness of sins, according to the riches of his grace.*"

Heb. 9:22—"*. . . without shedding of blood is no remission.*"

16. We were "purchased" and "reconciled" by the Blood?

Yes . . . . and here are the Scriptures to guide us.

Acts 20:28—"*Take heed . . . to feed the church of God, which he hath purchased with his own blood.*"

Col. 1:20—"*And having made peace through the blood of his cross, by him to reconcile all things unto himself; by him, I say, whether they be things in earth or in heaven.*

Verse 21—"*And you, that were sometimes alienated and enemies in your mind by wicked works, yet now hath he reconciled*

Verse 22—"*In the body of his flesh through death, to present you holy and unblameable and unreproveable in his sight;*

Verse 23—"If ye <u>continue</u> in the faith <u>grounded</u> and <u>settled</u> and be not <u>moved away</u> from the hope of the gospel . . . !"

I Pet. 1: 18-19—"For as much as ye know that ye were not redeemed with corruptible things, as silver and gold, from your vain conversation received by tradition from your fathers; "But [redeemed] with the precious blood of Christ, as of a lamb without blemish and without spot."

Verse 23—"Being born again, not of corruptible seed, but of incorruptible, by the word of God, which liveth and abideth forever.

Verse 25—". . . And this is the word which by the gospel is preached unto you."

17. We are made clean by the Blood?

I Jn. 1:7—"But if we walk in the light, as he is in the light, we have fellowship one with another, and the blood of Jesus Christ his Son cleanseth us from all sin.

Verse 9—"If we confess our sins, he is faithful and just to forgive us our sins, and to cleanse us from all unrighteousness."

I Jn. 2:2—"And he is the propitiation for our sins; and not for ours only, <u>but also for the sins of the whole world.</u>"

Rev 5:9—"And they sung a new song, saying, Thou art worthy to take the book, and to open the seals thereof; for thou was slain, and hast <u>redeemed us</u> to <u>God</u> by <u>thy blood</u> out of every kindred, and tongue, and people, and nation . . . !"

18. Sanctified by the Blood?

Heb. 13:12—"Wherefore Jesus also, that he might sanctify [set apart] the people with his own blood, suffered without the gate . . ."

Heb. 10:10—". . . . We are sanctified through the offering of the body of Jesus Christ once for all."

Heb. 10:19—*"Having therefore brethren, boldness [liberty] to <u>enter</u> into the holiest by the blood of Jesus.*

Verse 20—*"By a new and living way, which he hath consecrated for us, through the veil, that is to say, his flesh."*

Heb. 12:24—*"And to Jesus the mediator of the new covenant, and to the blood of sprinkling that speaketh better things than that of Abel."*

19. Is it Scriptural to "plead" the blood of Jesus in our prayers?

Yes! With the Blood, we have access to the Holy of Holies. No limitation for us in the heavenlies **(Heb. 12:24)!**

We come to God, plead our case; not relying on our works of righteousness but on the Blood for our justification. We are "justified" by His Blood!

The devil hates to hear us teach, preach, sing, about the Blood of Jesus.

God's mercy and forgiveness for us are eternally wrapped up in the Blood of Christ.

Devils cannot resist the atmosphere where the saints fully understand and appreciate the power in the Blood.

Deliverance, healing and miracle testimonies come up, because the Blood of Christ "speaketh" better things than that of Abel.

20. Isn't there so much disrespect for the Blood these days?

In some respects, yes. We counsel that the Blood should be approached with biblical reverence; for the Blood is holy.

Admittedly, there is unwholesome flippancy and ignorance exhibited by many who, at the slightest, excitement; scream "Blood of Jesus."

Yet, their ways do not measure up to the testimony of transformed lives.

It has become just a religious jargon or cliché in many charismatic circles.

Just as we would not take the Name of the Lord in vain; we should not take the Blood of Christ in vain. It should never become another ritual, peddled with unholy disposition and fanfare.

Many prayers are unanswered because of such misdirected practices.

The Blood "purchased" us from darkness and translated us into God's marvelous light. (Amen)!

We should never reduce it to a "mystical" word or "cliché" to be "chanted" by religious zealots. Indeed, there has been a lack of sound teaching on this subject in many places!

21. What of people who shout "the Blood of Jesus" at each other while quarrelling. Is this right?

No! It should never be.

As we have repeatedly emphasized, the Blood of Jesus is holy, and speaks of God's mercy, deliverance, healing, and access to God's throne and blessings!

The Blood must NEVER be "used" for vengeance; or to advance ill-will against perceived enemies!

Much of those practices come from the wrong teachings perpetuated by many so-called "deliverance" ministries who have abandoned sound biblical doctrine on the subject and gone after "fables!" **(2 Tim. 1:4; 4:7) (2 Tim. 4:4)**

The focus of their "deliverance" meetings is always on "enemies" and how the "believer" can "destroy" "adversaries."

22. Give an example how NOT to pray concerning enemies?

"Father, those my enemies who are against my progress in life, who don't want to see me succeed in my endeavors; who are against my destiny, O Lord, by your Holy Ghost fire, destroy them!

"Destroy them! Let their curses and blasphemies and evil desires return to them and their families! My father God, destroy my enemies.

Abba, let them cry and their tears be plentiful when they see me arrive at my destiny! (Amen)! Fire! Fire! Fire!

"I shout (Holy Ghost fire) . . . (Fire!) Upon my Enemies!

"Quench them, O God! Let them sink into the depths of the sea, into everlasting backwardness. Into Hell Fire!

I shout Holy Ghost fire (Holy Ghost fire!!!)

Fire!!! Burn them!!! "Destroy my Enemies! (Fire!!! Upon my Enemies in Jesus Name . . . Amen)!!!"

The above is an example of how you should NOT pray concerning your "enemies."

Yet, these are the kind of prayers going on in several "all-nights," "mountain-camps" and "fasting retreats."

"Ye know not the Scriptures nor the power of God."

23. What did Jesus teach about our enemies?

Mt. 5:43-48: *"Ye have heard that it had been said, Thou shalt love thy neighbor, and hate thine enemy.*

"But I say unto you, Love your enemies, bless them that curse you, do good to them that hate you, and pray for them that despitefully use you and persecute you"

"That ye may be the children of your Father which is in heaven; for he maketh his sun to rise on the evil and on the good, and sendeth rain on the just and on the unjust.

"For if ye love them which love you, what reward have ye? Do not even the publicans the same?"

"And if ye salute your brethren only, what do ye more than others? Do not even the publicans so?

"Be ye therefore perfect, even as your Father which is in heaven is perfect"

Rom. 12:14, 17-21

"Bless them which persecute you; bless, and curse not . . .

"Recompense to no man evil for evil . . .

"If it be possible, as much as lieth in you, live peaceably with all men.

"Dearly beloved, avenge not yourselves, but rather give place unto wrath; for it is written, Vengeance is mine, I will repay, saith the Lord.

"Therefore, if thine enemy hunger, feed him; if he thirst, give him drink, for in so doing thou shall heap coals of fire on his head,

"Be not overcome of evil, but overcome evil with good."

And the lord has spoken!

24. Will the blood of goats, ram, or cows save us from the dangers of life?

No! **Heb. 9:12-14** explains the reason.

"Neither by the blood of goats and calves, but by his own Blood [Jesus], He entered in once into the holy place, having obtained eternal redemption for us.

"For if the blood of bulls and of goats, and the ashes of an heifer sprinkling the unclean, sanctifieth by the purifying of the flesh:

"How much more shall the Blood of Christ . . . purge your conscience from dead works to serve the living God."

Col. 2:10—*"And ye are complete in Him . . ."* (Amen)!

CHAPTER 3

Deliverance and "Prophets"

25. Investigating family history in search of "generational" curses. Is this in the New Testament?

There is no such method in the New Testament.

None!

Any thorough study of the Gospels, Book of Acts, and the Epistles reveals the "psychological" approach, so popular these days was not even practised in the Scriptures!

Why? Because it is alien to the New Covenant!

Healing and deliverance, in the Gospels, come in answer to prayers. That's why it's called miracles of healing and deliverance.

Jesus did not "teach" investigating genealogies.

In other words, He did not investigate "generational curses." He did not tell us to; neither did the apostles in the Book of Acts.

Acts.1:1—*". . . . All that Jesus began both to do and teach"*

Apostle Paul warns the church about going into "genealogies" *(I Tim. 1:4)*—*"Neither give heed to fables and endless genealogies, which minister questions . . ."*

Titus 3:9—*"But avoid foolish questions and genealogies for they are unprofitable and vain!!*

All through the New Testament, there is no case of "genealogical" methodology in deliverance. And come to think of it, the pastor is not the healer or deliverer. The Lord is. (Thousands around the world are receiving true healings and deliverances from God through the simplicity of the gospel. Rather than bring healing, investigation of genealogies have often induced contentions, questions and further questions; malice and even hatred in families. God is not the author of confusion.

Come to Jesus as you are! He knows all about you already! You don't need to tell him any story about yourself. He doesn't need that help from you at all.

He is the Deliverer (waiting to save)! (Amen).

Throughout the Gospels, you don't see Jesus delving into generational curses in order to bring healing and deliverance.

He reveals the source . . . "the devil cometh not but to steal, kill and to destroy but I am come that ye might have life and have it more abundantly" **(Jn. 10:10).**

When the Lord sent the disciples out to the cities and villages, He didn't tell them to go investigating "genealogies". He told them to go preach the gospel!

Apostle Paul, in his missionary journeys, preached the Lord Jesus, the Savior who came to save the lost! Not once did he suggest the psychology—induced methods of some modern-day "deliverance" preachers!

Rather, Apostle Paul, seeing some worrisome trend in those days, warned against such rigmarole. **(I Tim. 1:3-4; I Tim. 3:9)**

We must follow the Master in His Example, "in all that Jesus began both to do and teach . . ." **(Acts 1:1)**

In the New Testament, you will not see such "investigations" about "genealogies," family curses" or "family history." None!

Let's release Holy Ghost power by "preaching" the "gospel," which is the power of God unto salvation, to everyone that believeth."

So, if all you preach is about "generational curses" and "genealogies"—it's time to go beyond that stuff and move on to the real simplicity of Jesus and His Cross!

Step into deliverance and cast out devils!

And if you are seeking deliverance, but you want some preacher to "divine" your family "curses" before you receive help, that is a wrong approach.

The Lord doesn't need you to go that route. He walked that road for you already!

He is the redeemer, carried your "curses," "sins" and "iniquities" on His own body on the tree, and by His stripes you are healed! **(I Pet. 3:24)** *Verse 25, "For ye were as sheep going astray, but are now returned unto the Shepherd and Bishop of your souls"*

Yes, in the past, before you became a believer (born-again); you were as sheep "going astray."

Apostle Peter reveals, you have now "returned" to who? To the Shepherd" and "Bishop" of your soul (Jesus)!

Think about that. This is purely an individual mandate. It's you and the Lord!

Have you "returned" to the "Shepherd" and "Bishop" of your soul?

Or are you still searching for "phenomena," "spirituality" and some form of "consciousness"?

Until you return to Jesus Christ (the Messiah), the void within you can never be satisfied!

Testimony . . .

The Word of the Lord came unto me . . . . (concerning this):

More than 15 years ago, (on a visit to Lagos), the Lord spoke to me (audible voice) while asleep in the night and gave me this revelation . . . : "Genealogies, Avoid."

I woke up immediately, and searched my Bible.

I knew He was telling me to "avoid genealogies" in the ministry of deliverance.

Genealogies should not be topical guiding issue in the Body of Christ! (Wisdom)!

Since then, I have endeavored to keep to the Scriptures, teaching and preaching the gospel, admonishing (whoever will listen), to return to the original gospel.

Walk away from the trumping of "generational curses" (without repentance and the Cross)!

(See my book, "Growing in Deliverance and Spiritual Warfare, Xulon Press, 2009).

26. Should prayer cloth, handkerchief and oil be used in ministration?

Yes, but should not be commercialized. They should not be sold. The church should NOT make "merchandize" of these items.

Acts 19:11-12—"And God wrought special miracles by the hands of Paul: "So that from his body were brought unto the sick handkerchiefs or aprons, and the diseases departed from them and the evil spirits went out of them!! Apostle Paul did not sell them.

27. Should I attend a "prophet's" ceremony to wash away my sins and troubles?

No ritual can wash away your sins and troubles.

Jn. 1:29—". . . *Behold, the Lamb of God which taketh away the sins of the world*" . . . *(Jesus Christ of Nazareth)!*

Jesus is the one you need. Receive Him into your heart and He will forgive your sins and lead you through life by His Spirit.

Mt. 11:28-30—"*Come unto me, all ye that labor and are heavy laden, and I will give you rest.*

"*Take my yoke upon you, and learn of me, for I am meek and lowly in heart; and ye shall find rest unto your souls.*"

"*For my yoke is easy, and my burden is light.*"

As the songwriter says:

"What can wash away my sins?
Nothing but the Blood of Jesus . . .
What can make me whole again?
Nothing but the Blood of Jesus . . ."

Get a gospel church that preaches "Born-again" (Salvation)! And stop dealing with the false prophet.

28. They are selling special stones and other blessed items from Jerusalem. Should we buy these to receive "favor" from God?

No. You should NOT buy so-called "blessed" "objects" in order to receive favor from the Lord. The grace of God is rich unto all who believe, whether Jew or Gentile. There is no difference. **(Rom. 12:12-13)!**

Beware of those who make "merchandise" of the gospel and mislead the unwary and simple-hearted.

2Pet. 2:1-3: *"But there were false prophets also among the people, even as there shall be false teachers among you who privily [privately, subtly, cunningly] shall bring in damnable heresies . . ."*

"And many [not few] shall follow their pernicious ways; by reason of whom the way of truth shall be evil spoken of (just as it is happening today)!

"And through covetousness shall they with feigned [swelling, exaggerated] words make merchandise of you . . ."

Jn. 2:6—*"And he said unto them that sold doves, Take these things hence; make not my Father's house an house of merchandise."*

(See Jn. 5:23-24)

29. I have been told to pay some money for blessing prayer! Is this biblical?

No! You don't have to pay money in order to be prayed for.

Prayers and blessings should not be for sale. Those who practice such methods enrich themselves and hold the people captive to their whims and caprices.

1 Pet. 5:2-3

"Feed the flock of God, which is among you, taking the oversight thereof, not by constraint, but willingly; not for filthy lucre, but of a ready mind

"Neither as being lords over God's heritage, but being examples to the flock."

2 Pet. 2:2-3

"And many shall follow their pernicious ways; by reason of whom the way of truth shall be evil spoken of."

"And through covetousness shall they with feigned words make merchandise of you; whose judgment now of a long time lingereth not, and their damnation slumbereth not."

30. If we pray for the sick, and do not see immediate result, what must we do?

Never give up!
Keep on believing!
Don't stop praying for the sick.

31. Am I supposed to wear "Bible verses" like "talisman" when I travel?

No. You are not to "wear" verses like "talisman."

Let the verses reside in your heart. Believe in your heart and declare the verses with thy mouth, and thou shall be saved.

The "unbelievers" like to "put on" things for "protection."

We are saved by the Blood of the Lamb and the word of our testimony!

Believe! **(Rom. 10: 6)**

32. I was told that suicide runs in my family. I'm now born again. Should I be scared?

You should not be scared! Jesus became the CURSE for you.

Walk in victory in Christ Jesus. Take a definite stand (in prayers) against that "spirit" of suicide. Rebuke it in Jesus' Name.

Speak to that spirit—it has no power over you and your family because you are now under the Blood!

The spirit of suicide needs to be cast out in Jesus Name!!!

Don't ever let fear come over you, concerning this evil.

You are free, and be not "entangled" again in the yoke of bondage. (Amen)!

If you are in the environment of good, biblical deliverance fellowship—get some honest prayer brethren (partners) to join you in such "violent warfare."

Remember, you have the victory!

33. In my country, olive oil is used only for "anointing" prayers. But I hear it is also very good for food. Is this true?

Yes. Olive oil is one of the most recommended by nutritionists.

34. Should we lay hands while casting out devils?

Not necessarily, but no hard and fast rule in Scripture. We can effectively cast out devils without the laying on of hands.

35. Do we cast out devils in our language or in tongues?

In our language! Not in tongues.

Devils know when superior authority comes!

For instance, an English-speaking believer can effectively cast our devils from non-English-speaking person.

Yet, the devils will obey and leave! In Jesus Name!

36. What special perfume or soap do I need, to enable me see visions when I pray or sleep?

You don't need any special perfume or soap or any other "accessory" to help you see "visions" As a child of God, you don't have to chase "visions" or "dreams." Instead, hunger and thirst for (Jesus), the word of God. **(Jn. 1:1).**

Religious "cults" and "mystical" fraternities indulge in such activities to induce "hallucinations," false "visions" and other (so-called) "esoteric" experiences.

The Holy Spirit is above all those satan-inspired (occult) experiences!

Seek the baptism of the Spirit and receive His gifts to glorify His Name.

37. Our pastor preaches that the only way we can bring the kingdom of God to earth is by getting actively involved in politics. All he preaches is politics. Is he right?

No, he is not right. The child of God should perform his/her civic duties. Your political persuasion should be your decision to make. The Body of Christ should not be compelled to support a particular political party. It is potentially divisive in the Body of Christ and deprives the people (believers) from thinking for themselves.

The kingdom of God is not synonymous with politics. It is far more than that. To insist it does, is a wrong teaching! Jesus still says "my kingdom is not of this world" **(Jn. 18:36)!** This subject is deeper than we can deal with here. The kingdom of God on earth is not equivalent to politics and the political world. It is different!

38. Is it true that eating only vegetables (no meat), makes someone more righteous?

Eating vegetables only, does not make anyone more spiritual in Christ. It is not what you eat or drink that makes you righteous in Him.

Rom 14:17—*"For the kingdom of God is not meat and drink; but righteousness, and peace, and joy in the Holy Ghost."*

For health reasons, one may avoid some kind of meat (or all meat products); but to ascribe that to righteousness is to trust the "works of the flesh" which is in itself "filthy rags" before God.

39. My pastor discourages us from reading books by other ministers of the gospel. Is he right?

No! He may genuinely be concerned about all kinds of teachings being put out by different authors.

However, he must not "throw out the baby with the bathwater."

Or he might just be paranoid about his church getting exposed to more balanced teachings than what he provides to his congregation.

Some church leaders make every effort to "bind" their "members" to themselves and not to Christ.

Get to a good Christian bookstore, check the books of your interest and feel free to buy and study. That is one sure way to grow. The Holy Spirit will lead and help you in your walk with the Lord. No matter how contended you may even be in your present church, avail yourselves the opportunity to benefit from the ministries of other men/women of God.

40. What are the special prayers we can pray to the angels for "special protections"?

There are no "special prayers" to be prayed to the angels. You should never pray to the angels. They are "ministering spirits" sent forth to "minister," (serve) us who are heirs of salvation!

Are you saved?

Christ is greater than the angels. The angels worship Him! **Heb. 1:6**—". . . . *and let all the angels of God worship Him*"!

1 Pet. 3:22 ". . . *Who is gone into heaven, and is on the right hand of God; angels and authorities and powers being made subject unto Him*"

False religious "cults" and "mystical" fraternities claim to have "patron" angels to whom they pray and seek favors!

All these bow to our Lord Jesus, because they are subject to Him. They are also subject to us in His Name **(Heb. 1:4)!** True angels of God are here to help us . . . . we must never pray to the angels or seek to know their names! No where in Scriptures does it tell us to pray to angels!

41. At a recent service, a woman of God brought the Word, sang and prophesied. But some people did not accept her because she is a woman. Do you think that was right?

No! We should receive whoever God has sent to bless the Body of Christ whether male or female (there's no difference)!

"There is neither Jew nor Greek, there is neither bond nor free, there is neither male nor female, for ye are all one in Christ Jesus." **(Gal. 3:28)!**

Apostle Paul mentions at least 7 women in

***Rom. 16—(Verse 1)**, Phebe, "a servant of the church which is at Cenchrea, that ye receive her in the Lord, as becometh saints, and that ye assist her in whatsoever business she hath need of you: for she hath been a succourer of many, and of myself also.*

***Verse 3**—Priscilla*

***Verse 6**—Mary*

***Verse 12**—"Salute Tryphena and Tryphosa who labour in the Lord. Salute the beloved Persis, which laboured much in the Lord"*

***Verse 15**—Julia and the "sister" Nereus.*

We should receive all who labour in the Lord, male or female!

CHAPTER 4
Prophetic Counsel

42. Explain Eccl. 10:19—". . . . Money answereth all things" Is this true?

No! Money does not answer "all things." Solomon's personal observation was on the behavior of men "under the sun;" man's earthly ways and circumstances!

"A feast is made for laughter, and wine maketh merry; but money answereth all things" It takes money to organize "a feast" This is true, even today.

However, we must not elevate Solomon's personal observation to the level of God's word, out of context. As someone has remarked, let us not take "a text, out of context, for a pretext" Why? Because we know that money does not answer "all" things.

Just because a bible character makes a statement does not necessarily mean that the statement is the complete Word of God. We are obliged to weigh such "verse" with other Scriptures especially those of our Lord in the New Testament.

". . . . A Greater Than Solomon Is Here (Lk. 11:31)
Did our Lord, in the Gospels, teach, affirm or even remotely advance the notion that "money answereth all things"?

Does the Book of Acts (of the Apostles) support Solomon's sweeping statement that "money answereth all things"?

Did the Apostles in the Epistles (Paul, Peter, James, John), directly or indirectly, teach us that "money answereth all things"?

Let's put some BALANCE in this subject, and look at the complete picture of the Scriptures.

Jesus Christ, the Messiah . . . is the One "greater than Solomon" who came (New Testament).

Money will not give eternal life.

That is one "thing" that money does not "answer." Money cannot buy salvation ". . . . the grace of God through faith **(Rom. 3:22-26).**

The "righteousness" which is of faith "speaketh" like this **(Rom 10:6-9):**

"Say not in thine heart, who shall ascend into heaven (that is to bring Christ down from above :)

In other words, don't say in your heart, "who will go to heaven and bring salvation for me; who will be my intermediary? Even if I have to pay money, or whatever it takes, who will get God's salvation and deliverance for me, who will bring God's anointing ("Christ is the Anointed one") down to me?

Apostle Paul says in this passage; don't even think like that "in thine heart."

Verse 7—*"Or, who shall ascend into the deep? (that is, to bring up Christ again from the dead)"* "don't even think of it. Who will go to the depths of the earth to bring up Christ again from the dead? But we know Christ is already risen from the dead! But some would prefer "works" as if Christ is not yet risen!

Their "religious" persuasions (in the church) anchor on depending on others to bring the "revelation" and "benefits" to them. Apostle Paul says, no! Don't fall into such delusion!

Verse 8—"But what saith it? (. . . the righteousness of faith acceptable to God):

"The word is nigh thee ["nearer to you than you realize, not far from you at all! You don't need to pay someone else to go get the word of the Lord for you")!

". . . even in thy mouth and in thine heart; that is the word of faith, which we preach;

Verse 9—"That if thou shalt confess with thy mouth the Lord Jesus, and shalt believe in thine heart that God raised him from the dead, thou shalt be saved.

Verse 10—"For with the heart man believeth unto righteousness; and with the mouth confession is made unto salvation." Money is not in the equation at all!

Money will not buy the Holy Spirit.

Money does not "answer all things" pertaining to the Holy Spirit and the gifts of the Spirit.

Acts 8:18-23—

"And when Simon saw that through lay on of the apostles' hands the Holy Ghost was given, he offered them money.

"Saying, give me also this power, that on whomsoever I lay hands, he may receive the Holy Ghost. But Peter said unto him, Thy money perish with thee, because thou hast thought that the gift of God may be purchased with money.

"Thou hast neither part nor lot in this matter; for thy heart is not right in the sight of God.

"Repent therefore of this wickedness and pray God, if perhaps the thought of thine heart may be forgiven thee.

"For I perceive that thou art in the gall of bitterness and in the bond of iniquity"

The people involved here were already believers, baptized in water and had received "great joy" in Christ **(verse 6-13).**

The great lesson (for today), particularly in Pentecostal/ Charismatic circles, is that spiritual experiences and blessings are not for the sole purpose of making money; nor for the purpose of making "merchandise."

Peter told Simon to "repent" from the "wickedness" of wanting to "purchase" the Spirit for personal gain. You cannot bribe your way with Jesus.

Jn. 3:3—*"Jesus answered and said unto him, Verily, verily I say unto thee, Except a man [rich or poor] be born again, he cannot see the kingdom of God"*

Let the Scriptures interpret Scriptures!

Money doesn't "answer" all things.

Study the balanced presentation of the Scriptures and "rightly" divide the word of truth!

2 Tim 2:15—*"Study to shew thyself approved unto God [not unto men], a workman that needed not to be ashamed, rightly dividing the word of truth."*

To "rightly" divide means to "set straight," to "present plainly without double talk, without equivocation. It means to give the true and concise meaning, in line with other Scriptures! That is, we must bring the Scriptures in agreement with other Scriptures.

To take a statement and jump overboard, making a doctrine out of it without due regard, study or consideration of the words of our Lord in the New Testament is clear invitation to error. And many errors are in the land! Finally,

1 Tim 6:10 admonishes—*"For the love of money is the root of all evil; which while some coveted after, they have erred from the faith, and pierced themselves through with many sorrows.*

Verse 11—*"But thou, O man of God, flee these things . . ."*

Solomon's wise conclusions:

Eccl. 12:13—*"Let us hear the conclusion of the whole matter; Fear God, and keep the commandments; for this is the whole duty of man.*

Verse 14 *For God shall bring every work into judgment, with every secret thing, whether it be good, or whether it be evil"*

A greater that Solomon is come! (Jesus Christ of Nazareth the only wise God and Savior) **(Jude 25)**!

43. "Heaven helps those who help themselves" Where is this verse in the Bible?

It is not a verse in the Bible. It's just a saying devised by men.

44. "If you move with the rich, you will be rich; but if you move with the poor, you will be poor; so don't fellowship with the poor." Is this in Ecclesiastes or Proverbs?

This is not even a verse in the Bible. Some flippant people devised the saying to justify themselves. The Bible says no such thing.

45. Is ecumenical "unity" the answer to Jesus' prayer that we all (believers) should be one?

No.

There were no "denominations" when our Lord prayed that prayer **(Jn. 17:21)**. His prayer was for believers (both Jew and Gentile), the two-people groups . . . (in that day); believers in Him (Messiah)!

He has broken down the dividing wall of hostility between Jew and Gentile! "Made us one" "new man" in Him! **(Eph. 2:14-16)**.

Again, the ecumenical "unity" group does not demonstrate true loyalty to the Lord Jesus.

46. Is the Name of Jesus Christ exalted in ecumenical gatherings?

The Lord told me,—"If the Holy Spirit is truly in the "unity," why is Jesus not exalted in those meetings? Why don't they lift Him up in their gatherings? By their fruits, ye shall know them!

47. Will there be one world religion with antichrist spirit?

Yes. They've been working on it for a long time. The United Nations is playing a crucial role in bringing it to fruition. Many Churches and other religions are involved; their agenda will be to bring world peace.

48. Can they really bring peace without the Prince of peace?

They will promise "peace," but it will be false peace! The conglomeration brings together world religions, council of churches, etc. ("brushing aside" our Lord Jesus)! False peace! Counterfeit worship! Outside the Messiah! Bible calls it "mystery, Babylon the great" because some good "ministries" (churches) are involved ("deceived" into the conglomeration, thinking it's God's will). This is prophetic!!! Come out of her, my people . . . **(Rev 18:4)**! He who hath ears to hear, let him hear.

Some great names (churches) are involved in this confederation (quietly).

The prophetic (eagle) eye has seen it all.

Watch (events) and pray (accordingly).

49. The Bible or Quran. Which came first?

The Bible came first!

50. Is it true that Christians and Muslims worship the same God?

Not true. The God of the Bible is not the "Allah" of the Quran.

51. Should we hate Muslims?

No. We should not hate anyone. The love of Christ is more powerful than hatred. As believers, we should endeavor to reach out with the gospel in the bond of peace.

52. Should we "recite" or "chant" names of angels in our prayers?

No. We must never "recite" or "chant" names of angels! False christs and false prophets are already gone into the world **(1 Pet. 2: 1-4); (1 Jn. 4:1-4)**!

Any "church" or "fellowship" that teaches such "pattern" of prayers is clearly in the "spirit of error" **(1 Jn. 4:6)**! Come out of such group, and get into a gospel teaching church where prayers are not through "angels."

53. In Lk. 17:32, the Lord said; "Remember Lot's wife." Why?

First let us briefly see how it was in the days of Lot . . . **(Verse 28)**

"Likewise also as it was in the days of Lot; they did eat, they drank, they bought, they sold, they planted, they builded,

"But the same day that Lot went out of Sodom it rained fire and brimstone from heaven, and destroyed them all"

Verse 30—*"Even thus shall it be in the day when the Son of man is revealed"*

And then in **verse 32**, the Lord commands us to "remember" Lot's wife!

On the way out of Sodom, she "looked back" contrary to the instructions (Word) and she turned to a pillar of salt! Disobedience (with impunity) brought immediate judgment to her.

Evidently, money and business dominated Sodom and Gomorrah with flagrant sexual sins, homosexual practices and complete disregard to God's laws!

It takes money to "eat, drink, buy, sell, plant and build—pleasures of sin were the main agenda of that society.

But the angels came with God's Word to warn Lot to get out (quick) with his family to escape the impending inferno.

Even though Lot's wife followed on, it soon became clear that her "heart" was still in Sodom!

Maybe she thought she had better "revelation" than the word of the Lord! The covetous and ungodly lifestyle of Sodom had stolen her heart!

Same today! Many in the church have heard the Word of the Lord for years! But the world still holds its grip on their hearts! "Sodom" has not left their "hearts"!

They think the sins of the world and Christ can go hand-in-hand! Lot's wife was supposed to believe and obey the Word that her husband followed!

We must be vigilant and not allow the temptations of the world to dominate our thinking and daily steps.

Hos. 6:3—*"Then shall we know, if we follow on to know the Lord . . ."*

The crucial test is not the beginning of Christian life and testimony.

Indeed, the critical challenge is in "following the Lord," in growing in His Word (personally)!

Lot's wife had a religious spirit which followed the crowd for a while but her pretence eventually failed the test. What the lord desires is your personal commitment to Him.

Jn. 14:15—*"If ye love me, keep my commandments"*

We may be very zealous in keeping the "commandments" of the church, but are we keeping His commandments?

Lot's wife received the same instructions not to look back. Yet, she did! That's clear disobedience! That same spirit afflicts the Body of Christ today.

Some are going back to the very worldly sins they rejected when they first got saved. They've allowed backslidden pulpit orators to persuade them that sin is no longer sin.

The main lesson for us (today) is to press in and not yield to the evil attractions of the world.

Remember, Lot's wife!

54. How can I know the will of God in my life?

The important thing is to know that God, in His infinite love and wisdom knows all about you. He knows all who are to be born when, where and how! He knows the name of everyone; He sees every detail of each person.

For example, He gave the name of King Cyrus 200 years in advance **(Is. 44:28)**. And His Word was fulfilled exactly! God knew about Jeremiah and the other prophets even before stepping into the dial of time to perform their callings. **(Jer. 1:5)**

The Bible also revealed about the coming of the "Messiah," "Emmanuel" (God With Us") centuries ahead of time.

But first, you must have the foundation of salvation and desire to grow in Him before desiring His will.

The true will of God is not to do your own will, but to do His will (in your life). That is the secret of true divine fulfillment! **(Jn. 7:16-17)**.

"Delight thyself in the Lord and lean not unto thy own understanding" **(Ps 37:4)** and that is the beginning of His will.

Mt. 7:21 declares, *"Not everyone that saith unto me, Lord, Lord, shall enter into the kingdom of heaven; but he that doeth the will of my Father which is in heaven"*

Some people wonder, many times, whether they are still in the will of God because of the trials and tests they are passing through.

Don't let satan mislead or deceive you or cause you to doubt God's infallible promises for your life.

Sometimes, it seems His promises are so far away. Remember, Joseph, in the Bible and all he went through.

Yet, God's promises never failed, even though men would have counted him out!

God will guide you in His pre-ordained plans! He will nudge you into His blessed paths! Trust Him **(Eph. 1:4, Eph. 2:20-22; Phil. 3:13-14)**

Even though you will have your hills and valleys, hold to your faith and don't yield to pressures from the unbelieving crowd!

God's will is revealed (as you walk daily in Him) and you will not walk in darkness! (Amen)!

55. Can we live in holiness these days?

Yes. But not in our own strength! However, we must be willing to submit, yield to His leading and discipline of His Word in our lives. In other words, we must determine to live for Him, to serve Him and do His bidding.

As a foundation, we must deliberately reject the lifestyle choices that bring us down from serving the Lord.

When our hearts are totally focused on the Lord, He will live the life through us . . . He who started the good work "in us" will "complete" it!

His purpose is that **(Lk 1:74-75):**

". . . . we being delivered out of the hand of our enemies might serve Him without fear,

"In holiness and righteousness before Him, all the days of our life"

We must move forward in our faith with confidence and the Lord will help us as we seek to follow unto holiness.

2 Cor. 7:1—*"Having therefore these promises, dearly beloved, let us cleanse ourselves from all filthiness of the flesh and spirit, perfecting holiness in the fear (reverence) of God"*

It is our responsibility to "cleanse" ourselves. It is an ongoing process. It is not a one-time shot at the last camp meeting or revival or last Sunday service!

You must be aware of the "filth" that invades both your flesh and mind and "cleanse" yourself. Avoid people and places that don't help your faith. Don't gamble with worldly lifestyles that "poison" your march to heavenly Jerusalem.

Again, note that there is "perfecting" process in holiness. So those who think holiness is impossible are wrong! And for those who say Christ has already made us holy, and yet live in sin, are not in the truth. Christ is NOT the minister of sin and unrighteousness! Old things are passed away in your life.

You must become a new creation in Him. **(2 Cor. 5:17).**

Eph. 4:24—

"And that ye put on the new man which after God is created in righteousness and true holiness"

Put on the new man (or woman) that you are; (created) in Christ. The new man, the new step (you must take) is waiting for you to "step into"—and live in it!

This is not about drawing up "rules" and "regulations"—abiding by men's definition of holiness!

Infact, this is not trivializing holiness as some are tempted to do!

You must walk away from "churchianity" into real serious business with our Lord and Savior! You don't need "revelations" from heaven to bring "holiness" down! You don't need "private interpretation" on holiness. Right now, you are to "put on the new man." Christ has done it all. Walk in it!

Forsake the evil attractions of the world. Is this possible? Yes!

1Thess. 3:13—

"To the end [purpose] he may stablish your hearts unblameable in holiness before God, even our father, at the coming of our Lord Jesus Christ with all his saints"

1Thess. 4:7—

"For God hath not called us unto uncleaness, but unto holiness"
He will not call you into something impossible for you.

Heb. 12:14—

"Follow after peace with all men, and holiness, without which no man shall see the Lord"

The Word (Scriptures) . . . ever so sure and steadfast! He gives you grace to live in holiness.

CHAPTER 5
Dreams, Visions & Revelations

56. What about Dreams, Visions and Revelations?

God still speaks through dreams, visions and revelations. This is a deep and fascinating subject, requiring balance, wisdom and understanding, especially in these (last of the) last days.

The Lord promised to "pour out" His Spirit upon all flesh, restoring prophecy, dreams, vision to both young and old, irrespective of gender **(Joel 2:28).**

True dreams, visions or revelations will not contradict the Word of God (in the Scriptures)! For instance, if you have a "vision" or "dream" or "revelation" instructing you to go to the beach or mountain or some "all-night prayer meeting" to pray for the death (elimination, or catastrophe) upon your "enemies", such dream or vision or revelation is definitely not from God. Why? Because God cannot contradict His Word.

Or if an "angel" brings some "doctrines" alien to the New Testament, that too should be ignored!

1Jn 4:1-

"Beloved, believe not every spirit, but try the spirits whether they are of God; because many [not few] false prophets are gone out into the world"

There is palpable confusion in many circles today because some in the church believe that once a "man or woman of God" teaches something (revelation?), then no-one should subject such declaration or revelation to biblical scrutiny.

Note the clear admonition, "believe not every spirit, but try (test) the spirits whether they are of God . . ." How? By weighing them side by side with the Scriptures!

But how can we "discern" or "try the spirits" if we ourselves are ignorant of the Word?

If you look at that Scripture **(1 Jn 4:1)** again, it doesn't say judge by the appearance of the preacher. Why is this important . . . ? Some "throw away the baby with the bath water" because the minister does not conform (either in dress or speech) to their religious traditions. Some will not accept anything unless it comes from their "apostle" or "bishop". That is plain ignorance!

We should "judge" visions, and revelations or interpretations given thereof.

57. Explain more about visions and revelations?

***Dan. 1:17* . . . .** *"And Daniel had understanding in all visions and dreams."*

"Visions" come in "mental pictures", dream, revelation; (definite word or insight) and you'll know it's . . . "thus saith the Lord! **(Dan. 9:20-23)**.

This can come in divine utterance, revealing, illuminating . . . **(Jer. 14:14-15)**. While asleep, visions can come clearly beyond the boundary of dreams! Visions and dreams can overlap in multiple dimensions.

Yet sight, appearance, like seeing something clearly with the eyes open, manifest in the realm of visions . . . **(Ezek. 1:1, 8:3)**.

All these manifestations from God "illuminate", "reveal" God's will and path, like light shining in the dark recesses of our lives or in the lives of others. What emerges is "revelation", because it comes from the Almighty, not "guess-work."

God can give you vision, dream or revelation affecting your life, or the life of a loved one or church. He can reveal what's ahead for the nation or nations or even small groups! Through anointed vessel, the anointing can both forth-tell and foretell.

You cannot limit Him . . . "And the Lord is that Spirit, and where the Spirit of the Lord (is Lord), there is liberty" **(2 Cor. 3:17)**!

When God sends visions or dreams, the ultimate purpose is to bring "revelation" on a subject or aspect of our lives. Yet, not all "revelations" come in the form of visions or dreams.

God's revelations often come through the Word (Scriptures) as one meditates or prays or fast or even as the believer goes about his/her daily activities. For instance, an inward witness (Word) can suddenly illuminate your spirit, building up your most holy faith to conquer your battles.

This could happen while you are taking a walk; at the barber's shop, or even taking a shower! (Wherever, whenever He chooses)! As the Lord wills!

58. What is the role of Scriptures?

While reading the Scriptures, the Holy Spirit can take a scripture and "reveal" it more to you; in the light of other scriptures. A divine understanding (help) accompanies such experience, exalting our Lord Jesus Christ and His Word. A true prophet brings the Scriptures (alive)!

In the Body of Christ, the revelation gifts, the word of knowledge, the word of wisdom and the discerning of spirits are manifested in the realms of the supernatural, edifying the assembly of believers.

Outside church gatherings; vision, dreams and "revelations" are to help us in our individual lives (when God decides); and to minister to others.

59. What are the Counterfeits?

We are not to seek "visions," "dreams" or "revelations" by praying to "angels." We must never pray to angels. Some false religious cults (that call themselves, "churches") encourage their "ministers" or "believers" to inhale some incense-type fragrance during "worship" and "meditation"-all to induce "visions."

60. Are there genuine revelations?

Yes. We don't want to give the impression that everybody out there is false.

But the tide of evil is rising fast and many large, anointed ministries (churches) know this is the truth. But they are silent and will not rebuke the manipulations of "fellow" ministers (because of "fellowship")!

61. Who will deliver the flock from "wolves in sheep's clothing?

Go back to the scriptures (Word) and don't be part of the "counterfeit" flow! Study "dreams," "visions" and "revelations" in both Old and New Testaments, and the Lord will give you understanding. You too, can walk in the light as He is in the light.

62. What else on dreams?

Not all dreams are messages from God. Many routine dreams are product of our imagination and daily experiences. They come through the "multitude of business" and over-indulgence **(Eccl. 5:3; Deut. 13:1-5, Jude 8)**!

Yet, the supernatural operates in dreams as God wills!

God spoke to the patriarch Abraham "in a vision" **(Gen. 15:1)** . . . . bringing the promise and the father of faith stepped up, looking forward to the promises!

God warned a pagan king, Abimelech, in a "dream" **(Gen 20:3)** to restore Sarah back to Abraham! Read the rest of the story **(Gen. 20:1-18)**!

63. What about Joseph's dreams in the Bible?

Perhaps, the most fascinating story concerns Joseph and his dreams! This young, gifted prophet, predicted his brethren would bow to him as revealed in his dreams.

They hated him for his audacity. Please note that Joseph's "dreams" were not his natural "wishes" or "ambitions" or what he "desired" for his "destiny".

Joseph did not "induce" his dreams. Rather, his dreams were divine, from God, supernaturally. When God gives you a dream, like he gave Joseph, you are not the author of that dream. It comes supernaturally. The fact that you may walk the path of persecution in its fulfillment doesn't mean that dream wasn't from God. God's supernatural dream is not "induced" or "inspired" by personal "greed!" The anointing of God was upon Joseph "for good!"

64. What lessons can we learn from Joseph?

Joseph was a "victim" of conspiracy by his "brethren," yet he was in God's perfect plan. Joseph was "mocked" as the "dreamer," yet he was in God's plan for his life.

Joseph was "physically abused," and "sold" to brutal slavery, while in the very midst of God's perfect plan!

Again, in Egypt, he could not escape "accusations . . ." he was jailed even though he was innocent. Today, in some Pentecostal/

charismatic ministries, they would have solidly maintained that Joseph was under a "curse."

They would have argued that the trail of "negative" "footprints" since his father gave him the coat of many colors was enough proof that, indeed, Joseph was under a curse! (. . . because all they preach today are "curses, curses, curses")!

This school of theologians, drunken with the dogma ("revelation") of "curses" in the Body of Christ would have been wrong then, as they are wrong today!

To interpret the believer's daily battles only in the prism of "curses" is alien to the New Testament.

Joseph was not under any curse when his brethren hated him! He was in God's perfect plan.

He was not under the curse when they sold him into slavery. Indeed, God was working out His plan!

This torpedoes modern theology. Joseph, prevailed (finally); not by his strength but by the favor of God, confirming his destiny, confounding the gainsayers! God was in it all "for good" (Amen)! **(Genesis chapters 37-48)**!

Many like to preach Joseph as Prime Minister of Egypt, (the glory of his latter end).

Please note that years before that, he suffered rejection, humiliation, loneliness, physical and mental anguish, yet his faith failed not!

Will you "endure" the process before the glory?

65. Are there counterfeits?

You must watch out for counterfeits.

► What are the "means" or "tools" used to receive the so-called "visions" "dreams" and revelations?
► What is the real message in the vision? Or dream?

▶ Does the "message" agree with the written Scriptures (Bible)?

▶ Does the "vision" promote man or does it inspire hearers to the path of discipleship in Christ?

66. How can we discern the right path?

Under the New Testament, the believer is not to yield to the spirit of confusion concerning these issues. When God reveals anything, whether in vision, dream or revelation, He will do it, distinctly. You will not need to run helter-skelter, searching for an interpreter. You don't need to buy a book on "interpretation" of dreams. If you dream a dream, and you don't understand it; pray that God would reveal the meaning to you. If He does, fine; if He doesn't, then move on with your life! A true minister can give you counsel and pray with you concerning your dream!

Don't let "anxiety" destroy your faith and joy in the Lord! We are not under the Old Testament anymore. Our Lord, by His Blood, has bought us . . . (redeemed) under the New Covenant, better than the old. "For in Him, we live, move and have our being" He is not far from us! He is not in some mountain, far away.

Again, you don't need to search for a "prophet or "prophetess" who will "help" you receive "visions" from God.

You don't need to pay money ("sow seed") in order to receive "visions" or "revelations"

If a "preacher," "bishop," "prophet," "prophetess" etc. demands money to "interpret" or "receive" revelation on your behalf then, that vessel walks not in the truth; is blind leading the blind!

Study the New Testament for yourself. Get a good Bible concordance and study "visions" and "dreams" in the New Testament and you will be amazed at the simplicity of God's Word. Delight in the Lord! You too can be a vessel in this area of ministry in these last days!

God still moves in "visions," "dreams" and "revelations." "Jesus Christ the same, yesterday and today and forever" **(Heb. 13:8)**! If you will pay attention, the Lord will lead you by His word, and revelation (Amen)!

67. I am not a very spiritual Christian. Can God speak to me in a dream?

God can speak to anybody in a dream. He is not limited in His outreach and counsel. He is the Lord of all flesh. Walk in faith. Study the Bible and live a simple Christian life.

Don't bother yourself if you have no dreams to talk about. Dream or no dream, the salvation of your soul is the most important. Listen to His inward voice in your spirit and obey His written word.

Seek the Lord, pray and study His word and He will lead you in all your ways. If you need a vision, dream or revelation, He will give it to you. But don't go from church to church, looking for "visions" or "dreams" for your life.

68. A "prophet" told me to move out of town to another city because (according to him) God has called me to minister there. Should I move?

Not just yet! Do you have a witness in your spirit that you need to move to another city for ministry? If God sent the "prophet" to you, wait for Him to confirm it also. Don't be hasty. We are in the New Testament!

But test the spirits if they are of God! If you have no witness, no testimony along the lines of the prophet's declaration, then be cautious. God is not the author of confusion.

Remember, you must always put God's Word ahead of man's. And when you are not sure, don't make any move. Keep praying and the Lord will guide you.

69. Do we need a "vision" or "dream" or "revelation" before we believe the Gospel?

No. We don't need a vision, dream or revelation to confirm the Gospel before we believe. Faith is believing God's Word as revealed in the death, burial and resurrection of Jesus Christ. The gospel is far superior to signs. The Word of God (Christ Himself) comes first before any vision, dream or revelation. When we hear the Word, we are to obey immediately! **(Heb. 3:7-8)!** **Jn 20:29**—"Jesus saith unto him, Thomas, because thou hast seen me, thou hast believed; blessed are they that have not seen, and yet have believed"

70. I dreamt that many people pursued me into a thick forest full of bees. Am I in danger? I'm born again.

You are not in danger. Rather, the dream is a spiritual wake-up call. You don't need to live in fear! But it's time to use your authority, as a believer, to pull down strongholds, and put the enemy to flight. The light of Christ in you is enmity against Satan's cohorts.
Eph.6:11—
"Put on the whole armor of God that ye may be able to stand against the wiles of the devil"
Stand up against the strategies of the devil. Pray always. If the Spirit moves you to fast, do so! If you have prayer partners in your church, give them the prayer request and boldly pray, "Pulling down" satanic strongholds who are determined to undermine your testimony in the Lord!
Please study **Eph. 6:10-18!**

When you pray, be bold! Why? Because our Lord defeated Satan at the Cross and gave us victory! The Blood of Jesus covers you and you are free indeed! (Also pray and fast as the Spirit leads)!

In the dream, you were trying to escape from these spiritual hoodlums. Now in reality, stand your ground. Don't run! Command them to turn back! (In Jesus Name)!

Pursue them! (With the shield of faith . . . . and "quench" all the fiery darts of the enemy)! "Resist the devil and he will flee from, you" Amen!

71. A visiting minister to our church prayed for everyone and "prophesied" spiritual gifts for almost everybody. What do you say?

Whoever prayed for you has come and gone. It's up to you to dedicate yourself to the Lord and be a true disciple indeed. **(Jn. 14:15)**!

Desire to be His vessel of honor and activate the gift within you.

"Seek ye first the Kingdom of God (Jesus) and His righteousness and all these things will be "added" unto you"

The laying on of hands by a minister can spark the gifts in you . . . . but how far you go in the Lord depends entirely on your dedication and faith. (No half measures)!

For instance, you can't just claim a certain spiritual gift and then go home (and sleep) so to speak; or go and live like the world!

- ► Delight thyself in the lord.
- ► Seek open doors to testify of His goodness.
- ► Be loyal to your Lord and Master, JESUS.
- ► Get close to Him (in thy chambers)!
- ► Read, Study His Word!

72. Many years ago, someone saw a "vision" that I was to go to a foreign country. I haven't gone anywhere since then. Was the "vision" false?

Not necessarily! If the Lord gave the "vision," it will come to pass! What was your "witness" of the "vision"?

Keep yourself busy; don't just sit idle, waiting for the fulfillment of the vision. Some visions take many years to be fulfilled!

73. Why is it that some ministers see "visions" all the time and others don't?

As for those who have "visions" "all the time, "my advice is, be careful. Ask yourself;

- ► Do they have the Word as much as they have "visions"?
- ► What kind of "visions" do they have?
- ► Do their "visions" lead to Christ?
- ► Do their "visions" lead to the Word of God (Bible)?
- ► Or do their "visions" glorify "problems" of the "hearers"?
- ► Do the "visions" glorify the "ministers' as "problem-solvers"?
- ► Do the "visions" encourage "materialistic life-style"?

Deut. 13:1-4;

"If there arise among you a prophet or a dreamer of dreams, and giveth thee a sign or a wonder,

"And the sign or the wonder come to pass, whereof he spake unto thee, saying, let us go after other gods, which thou hast not known, and let us serve them;

"Thou shall not hearken unto the words of that prophet, or that dreamer of dreams; for the Lord your God proveth you, to know

whether ye love the Lord your God with all your heart and with all your soul.

"Ye shall walk after the Lord your God and fear Him, and keep His commandments, and obey His voice, and ye shall serve Him and cleave unto Him."

74. Can a false prophet predict something and it would come to pass?

Yes! That a prediction came to pass should not be the only yardstick for us to accept a "prophet"! A false prophet is also "inspired" and often supported by supernatural sign or wonder! Such "prophet" would be the power of Satan. Don't forget the magicians in Egypt. **(Study Ex. 7:11, 22; 8:7, 18, Mt. 24:24)**

The real test of truth is not the display of signs and wonders but in the truth itself; the message, (Jesus is the way, the Truth and the Life)! False prophets don't have the light and can't give what they don't have! The truth is the Word of God as written in the Scriptures! They don't have the revelation of the Word!

75. Why does God allow false prophets to operate?

Heresies exist so that the truth will be manifested. Light must be manifested in the midst of darkness! **(1 Cor. 11:18-19; 2Jn 7-11)**! That's the reason God allows false prophets to be present.

76. We received invitation, to attend a Christian seminar where we would be taught how to receive visions and revelations from angels. Should we go?

There is nothing positive there! Don't get involved in such meetings! Stay with the Word on this subject of "visions," "dreams" and "revelations".

Refuse to be drawn into "fables" and "mystical spirituality" so-called! Stay with the Word of God which is the solid foundation of all truths!

Don't ever seek to receive visions, dreams and revelations from angels. (Even if some big names are involved in these seminars, don't go!)

Angels are ministering spirits, "sent" to "minister" for us who are heirs of salvation **(Heb. 1:14).**

God sends them and they minister for us. When we start "seeking" visions from them, we are treading on dangerous ground!

Many ministries have been shipwrecked by unbalanced focus on angels. You will appreciate this counsel in the days ahead. There are no such practices in the New Testament!

77. Are there prophecies that prayer can change?

Yes. These are called conditional prophecies.

(I) Hezekiah's life was lengthened even though Isaiah the prophet had given him a prophecy about his imminent death.

Isa. 38:1—"In those days was Hezekiah sick unto death. And Isaiah the prophet the son of Amoz came unto him, Thus saith the Lord, Set thine house in order for thou shalt die, and not live.

Verse 2—"Then Hezekiah turned his face toward the wall, and prayed unto the Lord.

Verse 3—*"And said, Remember now, O Lord, I beseech thee, how I have walked before thee in truth and with a perfect heart, and have done that which is good in thy sight. And Hezekiah wept sore."*

God had mercy on him and extended his life.

Isa. 38:4-5—*"Then came the word of the Lord to Isaiah, saying, Go and say to Hezekiah, Thus saith the Lord, the God of David thy father, I have heard thy prayer, I have seen thy tears; behold, I will add unto thy days fifteen years."*

Isaiah's prophecy was true. But Hezekiah's prayers reversed it and God's mercy prevailed.

(II) **Jonah 3:4**—*"Yet forty days and Nineveh shall be overthrown."* But the people of Nineveh responded to the preaching of prophet Jonah, *"proclaimed a fast"*, with the king leading a national repentance.

Verse 10—*"And God saw their works [of repentance] . . . ."* and Nineveh was spared.

78. Are there prophecies that prayer cannot change?

Yes. There are prophecies that prayer (and fasting) cannot change. These are called unconditional prophecies.

The Lord Himself gave some of the most profound unconditional prophecies.

(Mt. 24:4-42) (Lk. 21:8-36)—reveal such prophecies:

"Take heed that no man deceive you . . ."

"Many shall come in my name, saying, I am Christ, and deceive many . . . ."

". . . . Ye shall hear of wars and rumors of wars . . . ."

". . . . Nation shall rise against nation . . . Kingdom against Kingdom . . . ."

". . . . There shall be famines and pestilences and earthquakes in divers' places . . . ."

". . . . *And many false prophets shall rise, and shall deceive many.*

"*. . . And because iniquity shall abound, the love of many shall wax cold, But he that shall endure unto the end, the same shall be saved.*"

Prayers will not alter these prophecies.

Mt. 24:14—"*And this gospel of the kingdom shall be preached in all the world for a witness unto all nations; and then shall the end come.*"

Another prophecy that prayer cannot change:

The coming (again) of the Lord.

Acts 1:11—". . . . *Ye men of Galilee, why stand ye gazing up into heaven? This same Jesus, which is taken up from you into heaven shall so come in like manner as ye have seen him go into heaven.*"

This same Jesus, not another! (Amen)!

CHAPTER 6
Christian Life & Testimony

79. Who will not inherit God's Kingdom?

According to **Eph. 5:5**—*"For this ye know, that no whoremonger, nor unclean person, nor covetous man, who is an idolater, hath any inheritance in the kingdom of Christ and of God.*

Verse 6—*"Let no man deceive you with vain words; for because of these things cometh the wrath of God upon the children of disobedience.*

Verse 7—*"Be not ye therefore partakers with them."*

Verse 8—*"For ye were sometimes darkness, but now are ye light in the Lord; walk as children of light . . .*

Verse 11—*"And have no fellowship with the unfruitful works of darkness, but rather reprove them.*

Verse 12—*"For it is a shame even to speak of those things which are done of them in secret."*

"Whoremongers"—Greek ("pornos") male and female prostitute, "pornography"

"Fornicator," . . . "them that defile themselves with mankind; **(1 Tim. 1:10)**!

". . . . Unclean persons . . . . Greek ("akathartos"), homosexual, perverts,

". . . addicted to luxury, sexual vice and subdued prostitution"

Warning: Anyone engaged in these lifestyles will NOT inherit the kingdom. God is no respecter of persons!

80. Why are some people always going for deliverance and never seem to be delivered?

Reasons may differ on case by case basis. However, the main explanation could be that many who come for deliverance are looking forward to the ritual, the routine, the prayer, and the preacher.

They are not looking to Jesus the Lord but rather to the problem, the enemy and the pressures of life around them.

Again, the preachers who focus only on "deliverance" and fail to teach the complete Gospel to humble seekers, are part of the problem.

"Unforgiveness" is the most serious impediment to total deliverance . . . (Whole-man healing)!

Many come for "deliverance" but are not willing to live for the Lord. They want to go back and live like the world. They enjoy their sins and iniquities! But the mercies of the Lord still endure. The Lord Jesus is still in deliverance.

81. Is it right for Christians to be members of secret societies (Cults)?

No! Christians should not belong to secret societies.

2 cor. 6: 14-18—*"Be ye not unequally yoked together with unbelievers; for what fellowhsip hath righteousness with unrighteousness? And what communion hath light with darkness?*

Verse 15—*"And what concord hath Christ with Belial? Or what part hath he that believeth with an infidel?*

Verse 16—*"And what agreement hath the temple of God with idols? For ye are the temple of the living God; as God hath said, I* *will dwell in them, and walk in them; and I will be their God and they shall be my people.*

__Verse 17__—"Wherefore come out from among them, and be ye separate, saith the Lord, and touch not the unclean thing; and I will receive you,

__Verse 18__—"And will be a Father unto you, and ye shall be my sons and daughters, saith the Lord Almighty."

82. We don't have Bible Studies in my church. How do I study the Bible?

There are many good publications in Christian bookstores which can help you study the Scriptures in a more personal way. Check any Christian bookstores for such publications.

83. How can I develop myself in the gift of prophecy?

By praising the Lord! Worship Him. Read and Study His Word. Love Him. Surround yourself with, and, soak yourself in His songs, worship and praises! Lift Him up! (JESUS)!

84. How do I know God's voice?

You have to know the Written Scriptures. That way, you'll be familiar with His Word. His voice speaks His Word.

It's going to take you some time walking with the Lord (experience) to know when He is speaking to you.

- ▸ Seek Him more than silver and gold!
- ▸ Read the Scriptures (New Testament) to begin with and you'll get used to the voice of Jesus!!!

85. Did God create other worlds?

Yes, of course! **(Heb.1:3)** ". . . . by whom also He created the worlds" (plural)! Christ (as the "Everlasting Father") created the universes and man is still busy, trying to figure out His vast creation.

Col. 1:16—"for by Him, were all things created, that are in heaven, and that are in earth, visible and invisible, whether they be thrones, or dominions, or principalities, or powers: all things were created by Him and for Him."

86. How can I grow in the Lord?

- ▸ By studying the Bible.
- ▸ Getting involved in church activities.
- ▸ Stop the old life of worldliness
- ▸ Seek those things which are above (Supernatural)
- ▸ Pray and commit your daily life to Jesus our Lord!
- ▸ He will lead you!

87. As a Christian student, should I study evolution or just ignore it.?

Study it, like you would study any other subject.

88. Some people can pray for hours but I can't. Do I have a problem?

Not necessarily. Walk in the grace, God has given you. Keep praying.

89. Our church doctrines come from the Old Testament and "visions" of our founder. What's wrong with that?

We are in the New Covenant established by the Blood of Christ. We are no longer under the Old Testament ordinances and laws.

Therefore, operating under the old with the founder's "visions" puts the congregation in another kind of bondage, in darkness, not knowing the Word of God, not knowing the Gospel which is able to set us free.

The New Testament is the key to the church of Jesus Christ!

CHAPTER 7

Homosexuality

90. What does the Bible say about homosexuality?

The Bible condemns homosexuality as sin.

Lev. 18:22—"*You shall not lie with a male as one lies with a female, it is an abomination.*"

1 Cor. 6: 9-10—"*Know ye not that the unrighteous shall not inherit the kingdom of God? Be not deceived: neither fornicators, nor idolaters, nor adulterers, nor effeminate, nor abusers of themselves with mankind [i.e Greek . . . "arsenokoites"—"one guilty of unnatural offences; sodomite; homosexual; sex pervert . . .*"];

Verse 10: "*Nor thieves, nor covetous, nor drunkards, nor revilers, nor extortioniers, shall inherit the kingdom of God.*

Verse 11: "*And such were some of you: but ye <u>are washed,</u> but ye <u>are sanctified,</u> but ye <u>are justified</u> in the name of the Lord Jesus and by the Spirit of our God.*"

Rom. 1:26—"*For this cause God gave them up unto vile affections: for even their women did change the natural use into that which is against nature.*"

This refers to lesbianism—"unnatural sexual relations between women" (homosexuality)!

Verse 27—"*And likewise <u>also the men,</u> leaving the natural use of the woman, burned in their lust one toward another; <u>men with</u>*

men, working that which is unseemly, and receiving in themselves that recompence of their error which was meet."

This, again, refers to sodomy or homosexuality.

(Other references: 2 Tim 3:3, 13
2 Pet. 2:7-22
Jude 7-19)

91. What option, then, for a homosexual who wants to abandon such "lifestyle"?

Just like every other sin (as the Bible defines it), there is forgiveness and redemption for anyone who comes to our risen Lord Jesus. If you come to the Lord, as they came in Bible times, with faith, your "lifestyle" will be dealt with supernaturally in a truly "born-again" deliverance experience.

But you must accept what the Bible calls it . . . . "sin" and "repent"!

In the early church, there were those who had lived the homosexual lifestyle before being saved and redeemed.

1 Cor. 6: 11—*"And such were some of you: but ye <u>are now washed</u>, but ye <u>are now sanctified</u>, but ye <u>are now justified</u> in the name of the Lord Jesus and by the Spirit of our God."*

"Washed" by the Blood of Jesus! <u>"Sanctified"</u> by the Blood! "Justified" by the Blood! Walking in the newness of life in Christ Jesus. This is not what others can decide for you. You have to decide for yourself.

92. Is the Bible view of homosexuality, hate speech?

No.

Stating the Bible position on homosexuality does not mean that we hate those who are gays and lesbians.

The Gospel of Christ is message of love, which calls us all to the altar of repentance on every issue that the Bible calls "sin," Homosexuality is not the only sin in the Bible. There are numerous other sins.

Repentance is the key, the first step!

The pathway to redemption remains the same for every sin.

Repent and believe the gospel!

The gospel does not advocate hatred towards those who live the sodomite lifestyle.

Yet, for those of them who seek redemption in Christ, and accept the Bible classification of that lifestyle as sin, there is promised grace and spiritual enablement to abandon homosexuality.

93. Is the Bible position politically correct?

No.

The Bible view of homosexuality as sin is not politically correct.

Contemporary popular culture, promoted by political, social, media and judicial authorities tend to label those who honestly disagree with the pro-gay crowd, of homophobia.

Their agenda is to orchestrate the pro-gay and lesbian momentum with sweeping intolerance, for which they accuse those who disagree with them.

To openly state the Christian viewpoint now, is to invite being branded as "bigot," "narrow-minded" and "intolerant."

Yet, media coverage give distorted impressions as if the opposing views are only "hate-speech" rhetoric.

Support for gay-rights, in many liberal-leaning constituencies, is the commonsense option for many a politician eyeing the next election (here in the USA)!

Saying what the Bible says will not always be popular and politically correct because the world is running on its wheels that are anti-Christ in spirit. And that should not surprise us.

Even so, we must continue to reach out to those outside our walls. We must continue to resist every attempt to railroad pro-gay and lesbian agenda down our throats.

We, too, have the right to disagree. That is a right guaranteed by the United States Constitution.

94. Is there a Gay "Bible"?

Yes.

They have changed many passages in the real King James Version and they call theirs "The Queen James Bible." There may be more versions of their "bible" coming out later.

Clearly, the "Queen James Bible" is a perversion.

The anonymous editors of "QJB" have produced their Gay-friendly "bible."

An example: (The King James Version) **Lev. 18:22**—*"Thou shall not lie with mankind, as with womankind: it is an abomination"*

(The Queen James Version)—*"Thou shall not lie with mankind as with womankind <u>in the temple of molech</u>; it is an abomination."*

As you can see, "in the temple of Molech," is their own addition, to promote their sexual preference, their sexual agenda.

The implication of their "translation" is that homosexuality is permissible outside the "temple of molech."

This is a clear case of prejudicial translation!

What will those lukewarm churches say about this?

CHAPTER 8
Chrislam

95. What is "Chrislam"?

Chrislam is an effort by Christian and Muslim entities to bring together Christianity and Islam in blended form of worship and practice. The main focus of its proponents is that one can be a Muslim and at the same time be a Christian; and vice versa. It seeks to minimize the differences between Christianity and Islam.

Advocates of Chrislam enthusiastically refer to the fact that Jesus is mentioned 25 times in the Quran.

96. What is wrong with Chrislam?

The truth is that Christianity and Islam are opposites in their basic premises of faith, doctrine and practice. Therefore, a blending, which Chrislam represents, dilutes and denies the very essentials of Christianity.

The Bible declares that Jesus Christ of Nazareth is God incarnate, God "manifest in the flesh" **(1 Tim. 3:16)**. The deity of Christ is at the root of Christian belief. Why? Because, without His deity, Jesus' death on the cross would not atone for "the sins of the whole world" **(1 Jn. 2:2)**.

As for Islam, it vehemently rejects the deity of Christ. The Quran declares the idea that Jesus is God to be blasphemy. Again, Islam denies the death of Christ on the cross.

Therefore, Chrislam should be rejected by every true believer in Christ.

97. How widespread is Chrislam?

It is spreading . . . . and many notable churches and ministers are its advocates. The list will surprise you!

In some churches (already), Qurans are placed next to Bibles in the pews, Sunday school lessons and sermons on Mohammed, the founder of Islam, are common place.

These congregations have spread as far wide as Houston, Atlanta, Seattle, Detroit and other cities.

Chrislam has, indeed, gone far since it was founded in Nigeria in the 1980s.

The tide of Chrislam might come knocking at your (church) door, soon!

Beware!

Watch and pray!

CHAPTER 9

The Moving of the Spirit

98. How do we discern if it's the Holy Spirit operating?

The Holy Spirit exalts and glorifies Jesus Christ, the Messiah.

The Holy Spirit will "reprove the world of sin, and of righteousness, and of judgment."(Jn. 16:8).

The Holy Spirit will lead sinners to Jesus, the Christ and establish believers into the maturity of faith (Eph. 4:8-16)

99. Are personal talents the same as "spiritual gifts" of 1 Cor. 12?

No.

Personal talents are not the same as "spiritual gifts" of 1 Cor. 12: 1-31.

These gifts are supernatural.

100. How can we know if a revival is God-sent?

A true revival is when Jesus Christ is exalted, above all.

The Word of God is given prominence beyond everything else . . . and the moving of the Spirit (evident).

Salvation is preached . . . sinners, saved and the joy of the Lord comes, uniting His saints!

Moreover, any God-sent revival will bring love among God's people . . . and the supernatural manifesting in diverse gifts (1 Cor. 12) to the glory of God!

CHAPTER 10

Testimonies

————⊶⊷————

1. After the Salvation-Healing Crusade that night, the young girl looked up and by her bedside, to her right, was an angel, "mending" her ribs which had made her bedridden for sometime. When the angel disappeared, the young girl regained strength and knew she was healed. Next morning, she asked for real good breakfast, instead of her liquid "diet" earlier prescribed by the doctor. She narrated her experience to her parents.

   They took her to the doctor who confirmed she was completely healed.

   Another young man reported, days after the Crusade, that he was completely healed of a

   cancerous sore in his right leg. He said, during the "casting out of devils" ministration, he felt like "stones" shooting out of his open sore. A few days later, he was completely whole. Praise the Lord!

————⊶⊷————

2. Woman walked up and down the aisle freely, happy, testifying that she was light and moving without hindrance. She said, she always felt her legs couldn't carry her weight.

But that night, as I called her out, she walked, demonstrating her miracle before everybody.

———⸻———

3. Woman (alcoholic), brought by her friends and relatives to the meetings. The spirit of alcoholism was cast out and there she was on the floor, without me laying hands on her! She remained on the floor, rest of the service. When she got up, finally, she was delivered!

———⸻———

4. This was an emergency call from Nigeria. Mama had been involved in an auto-accident and had been in coma.

From the University of Benin Teaching Hospital, she was being transferred to Ife University Teaching Hospital.

Over the phone, we ministered "prayer cloth" healing to be taken to Ife that morning!

In about 3 days, when I called to check, she was already in Benin, taking care of grand kids! (Amen! To the Lamb of God)!

We were all amazed by the miracle. Till this day, Mama does not cease to offer thanks and praises to "Jesu n'ogie" (Jesus, the King)!

There is no distance with God! Across the Atlantic or Pacific, He's always just the same!

———⸻———

5. She requested appointment for prayers: for herself, business and her family issues.

Before the appointed day, the Lord told me, she had serious medical issues which she didn't mention. At the appointed time, I told her that she had medical problems she didn't mention.

She confessed that she had a litany of medical issues . . . etc.; and that she just returned from a visit to her doctor.

I ministered to her through the Scriptures and prayed for her.

"What God reveals, He will heal" (Amen)!

———— ✺ ————

6. "We appreciate your 4-week Mission-trip, teaching and preaching in our "Jamaica Revival Explosion." We are encouraged by your dedication, humility and passion for the Lord and His prophetic message of truth and deliverance. You have been a blessing to all of us in Jamaica."

—Bishop Joseph Ade-Gold (Ph.D.).
Overcomers World Ministries, (Kingston, Jamaica.)

———— ✺ ————

7. "I do not know where to begin . . . you have shown us that God requires obedience—no matter how inadequate we may feel."

L.D—(Kingston, Jamaica)

———— ✺ ————

8. "Thank you for obeying the Lord and coming to us. I have been blessed and encouraged by you."

M.J.—(Kingston, Jamaica)

———— ✺ ————

9. "Your teaching of the Word is very simple, yet sharp and powerful . . . excellent Word-based ministry."

M.W—(Kingston, Jamaica.)

10. "Earlier that week, a brother had spoken to me about the spirit of fear. So I was surprised, when your message tonight was on "Deliverance from the spirit of fear."

    I was truly blessed by your message . . . prophetic and powerful. It changed my life."

    Sis. K—Mandeville (Manchester), Jamaica

11. "For the past few days, I was under the spell of fear. Even today, I was fearful throughout. Then, I came to the service and you boldly preached on "deliverance from the spirit of fear. I stepped forward in the altar call. Thank God for His Spirit. Praise the Lord."

12. "I have more freedom (now) to pray after being in your meetings"

    Sis. S.—(Kingston, Jamaica.)

13. "Great service! Deliverance Rally-Prayer Line. Confronting and casting out occultic spirits, in Jesus Name."

    —Sis. D—(Portmore, Jamaica.)

14. Giving exhortation to a small group of believers and invited guests, I called out those who just couldn't sleep at night.

At first, what I said sounded "out of place", "out of order" . . . until one hand went up, then another, and another etc. All of them stepped forward . . . .

Again . . . "What God reveals, He heals"!

15. This lady had had immigration problem for years . . . . Things had gotten messy and complicated.

    Now, they invited her for "interview". When she told me, I assured her not to fear, because they would grant her desires!

    "Don't worry about it, because you will get your green card, this time around"!

    She did! (Praise the Lord)! She testified to others what the Lord had done!

16. "When (Pastor) Andrew, suddenly, called me from America, he gave me the word of the Lord. (I hadn't spoken to him for years) . . . and told of the travails I was going through in my office . . . and prophesied that nothing would shake me (out of that place) . . . that I should rejoice, praise the Lord and would see the salvation of the Lord!

    It's been years, what (Pastor) said, happened exactly.

    I'm still here, moving higher and the detractors, put to shame! O, praise the Lord!"

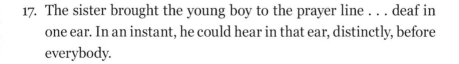

17. The sister brought the young boy to the prayer line . . . deaf in one ear. In an instant, he could hear in that ear, distinctly, before everybody.

Somebody says how do you know he was healed of his deafness?

The healing was demonstrated before the entire audience to see and verify. Amen!

18. "When you called out (ministers and all) who desired a deeper walk with the Lord, I stepped forward. I didn't go to work that night because I wanted to be in the meeting. You prayed and prophesied!

I want to report that my life was greatly imparted. I, now, have real zeal for God and His work. My understanding of the Scriptures has taken on new meaning and our business which has been dormant is rising again. Thank God for your life."

Sister B. (Dallas, TX).

19. "The Holy Spirit was moving, after I preached on the Baptism of the Holy Spirit . . . and many came forward to receive the baptism. As the people, prayed, rejoiced and worshipped, tongues and prophecies burst out from the new recipients at the altar.

One particular sister, from out of town, prophesied more than them all . . . . and something else surprised us. She called on the organizing pastors to throw away the anger and bitterness among them, to forgive one another . . . . reconcile among themselves because the Lord was ready to bless His people!

What a shaking! After that morning session, the ministers got together, and confessed one to another. You could feel the glory of the Lord. The ministers of the Lord took the prophecy seriously and did accordingly! (Praise the Lord)!

20. And now, here is the **star-witness:**

Many years ago, coming to work at the Editor's Desk (The Observer, Benin City, Nigeria), I heard the voice of the Lord (audibly) to leave the place that morning.

I felt the anointing confirming same. Quickly, I obeyed and submitted my voluntary retirement application to the General Manager in less than 10 minutes. (Time was about 8:15am). In less than an hour, Nigeria's military government ordered the closure of the Observer newspaper.

Technically, I was already out of the place! Many of my friends and colleagues always wondered how I left . . . just at the nick of time. Well, you know the answer (now) . . . .

Praise God!!

PROPHECY

I see a mighty wave and move of the Spirit
Bringing deliverance to the captives.
Tears of joy roll down faces of multitudes
As God's grace and mercy sweep through burdened souls.
O, what liberty! What freedom!
The yoke of bondage weighed down these
captives—and many waited.
What load is this?
What oppression is this?
For years and years, Satan's load of cares weighed heavily
on these multitudes, stretching far, far as the eye can see.
Suddenly, the cry of the Name of Jesus Christ!
And the yoke is broken . . . the chains are broken!
Like New Wine, each soul is sweetened by His love divine!
The spoken Word opens the veil of His presence
And multitudes drink of His living water!
O blessed be this hour!
Exalted and magnified is His Holy Name . . .
And consumed in this Holy Banquet are multitudes
who partake of His glory and grace.
Everything else counts as naught.
Only His name, His name
Is worthy to be praised!!! (Amen)!